UNTIL WE FIND EACH OTHER

Brooke Berman

BROADWAY PLAY PUBLISHING INC
224 E 62nd St, NY NY 10065-8201
212 772-8334 fax: 212 772-8334
BroadwayPlayPubl.com

UNTIL WE FIND EACH OTHER
© Copyright 2010 by Brooke Berman

First printing: June 2010
I S B N: 978-0-88145-456-7

Book design: Marie Donovan
Typographic controls & page make-up: Adobe InDesign
Typeface: Palatino
Printed and bound in the U S A

UNTIL WE FIND EACH OTHER received its world premiere at Steppenwolf Theater Company in Chicago, directed by Anna D Shapiro. It was developed at Steppenwolf, at the Eugene O'Neill Theater Center in Waterford, CT, and in New York City through Rising Phoenix Rep, The M C C Playwrights Coalition and New Dramatists. Its early development in New York was funded by a grant from the National Foundation for Jewish Culture, and the play was initially directed by and developed with the invaluable Linsay Firman.

And it shall come to pass afterwards that I will pour out My spirit on all flesh; your sons and your daughters shall prophesy, your old ones shall dream dreams and your young people shall see visions.
Joel 3:1

...while tribes do allow for a certain sense of warmth and connection, they ultimately cost us more than they give us in a modern, cooperative global culture,"
Douglas Rushkoff

The Kabbalah, teaches us that galut, "exile", is the fundamental reality and pain of existence... It teaches that one of the causes of the exile is the alienation of the masculine from the feminine in God...[and]that each of us can effect the overturning of galut by dedicating all our efforts to the reunification .... When the masculine and feminine aspects of God have been reunited and the female half of humanity has been returned from exile we will begin to have our tikkun *("reparation").* The world will be repaired.
Rita M Gross, **Female God Language in a Jewish Context**

PRODUCTION NOTE

In both workshop and production, we staged this play, as with most of my work, without scene breaks—each piece moving seamlessly into the next, as if collaged together, pushing the story forward. Thus, the pieces, while noted separately, by number, should not be treated as separate "scenes". Sometimes, we spoke of the disparate elements of and characters in the play affecting each other like a pinball machine— the silver ball launches on its journey, crashes into everything it meets, and catalyzes a great, connected series of actions. If one can imagine Sophy taking a big mouthful of pills before the story starts – that might be the silver ball. Or perhaps the silver ball is the invocation, or prayer, of the prologue, creating sacred space.

The play is deliberately structured in kaleidoscopic and accumulative movements. Scenes can and should overlap. The playing space should have movement to it and reflect the interconnectedness between the thoughts, needs, and memories of the characters. Everything is connected to everything else, everyone too. It a pulsing, holographic Universe. This is why Steve comes back at the end.

We also discovered that it made a great deal of sense for Sophy to be physically present on stage throughout the play, as if watching and motivating her cousin's actions.

The tone is straightforward and bright, even funny. There is a buoyancy to its rhythms, even when these rhythms dip into the moody depths. The play should take us on a ride.

CHARACTER NOTES

Although Justin, Miriam and Sophy are psychic—and wrestle, to different degrees, with their respective psychic gifts—they should be recognizable, contemporary, funny and self-aware young people. They are passionate, intelligent and restless – but not, as Sophy insists, lost souls. She in particular should not feel like a lost soul or lost cause. By the time we meet Sophy, it's as if she has collected each of her past selves, accumulated and them so that she can participate in the story and also, propel her cousins forward. We should never feel that she's damaged or crazy.

There may be a stylized or anachronistic element to her costume. In the New York workshop, we staged her wrapped in Christmas lights around an old trench coat. In the Chicago production, she wore a headscarf and coat but beneath that, a sparkly dancer's leotard and fishnet stockings. She is a character who exists in and belongs to more than one world or level of experience.

There is a delight in performing for SOPHY, a delightfully per formative quality to her monologues with the audience. As if she gets this one Greatest Hits Tour before she returns to the ether, to be renewed as a post-death soul. Death is not a bad/tragic thing for her or in the world of this play. The play holds no judgment on her choice. SHE should be visually integrated with the rest of the play, although her rules of movement must be specific to the rules of a soul in transition.

Her physical presence and effect on Miriam is palpable.

Prologue

(Lights up on the three. They address the audience. The prologue is both direct and clear.)

SOPHY: *Baruch Ata Adonai—*

MIRIAM: Blessings. For Ye on the Road.

SOPHY: *Elohenu Melech Ha'Olam—*

MIRIAM: Sanctified be thy road trips—

JUSTIN: This is what I see. It's from the past: Three cousins. Two girls. a boy nearby. He spies on them. they run away. He climbs a tree. He watches them. He falls out of the tree. *(Not his fault)* One of the girls runs away to smoke a cigarette she's found in her mother's bag. The other girl and the boy go back up the tree and watch the whole world. It's green, the whole world. They tell each other they will never be apart. this is not said. it is understood.

SOPHY: Blessed art thou, O Lord Our God, who points us in the direction of tikkun olam—

JUSTIN: The healing of the world.

MIRIAM: Who lets us see the freeway in the dark, who points us in the direction of all the good detours—

SOPHY: Who helps us find each other, whenever we need to, again and again.

(They move into the first scene of the play.)

One

(MIRIAM *and a lover. They are in her truck driving North.
His name is* STEVE. *He fiddles with the radio. Passes
N P R* All Things Considered. *Chooses fiddle music. They
have been driving for a while.*)

STEVE: Where are you going?

MIRIAM: Following signs.

STEVE: What signs? Road signs?

MIRIAM: Signs in my head. Dreams. Impulses.

STEVE: Sure.

MIRIAM: Messages—

STEVE: Sure.

MIRIAM: From my cousin sometimes.

STEVE: Oh.

MIRIAM: *(Very matter of fact here)* My mom died a year
ago. I left.

STEVE: I'm—

MIRIAM: *(She cuts him off; doesn't want him to say he's
sorry)* Where are you from again, Steve?

STEVE: Texas.

MIRIAM: Did I know that?

STEVE: I don't know. Didja?

MIRIAM: I don't know.

STEVE: Yeah.

MIRIAM: Know who I'm named after?

STEVE: No.

MIRIAM: Miriam.

STEVE: Yeah?

MIRIAM: From the Bible.

STEVE: I don't know who that was.

MIRIAM: The older sister of Moses. And she was a
prophet. God struck her down with leprosy because,
well the story is complicated but essentially she said
that Moses wasn't the only one who could talk to
God. She said she was talking to Him all the time,
getting messages too. And no one liked that she said it,
anything against Moses. So God gave her leprosy. Then
He forgave her. Moses asked Him to. After that she
just, like, made music. Interestingly enough, later on,
Jesus would essentially make the same point. Or close.
He said the kingdom of God is within. Go within.
Have your own direct experience of God. All the great
prophets—the Buddha, certainly—have discovered,
dis-covered—that you can access it—in the human
experience—without a middleman—a guy in between.
Anyway, we don't know what really happened and
what was just bad translation and propaganda.

STEVE: You're Jewish?

MIRIAM: Yeah.

STEVE: Oh.

MIRIAM: *(Teasing him)* Know a lot of Jews, Steve?

STEVE: Not really.

MIRIAM: There are Jews in Texas.

STEVE: Not Abilene.

MIRIAM: Point taken.

STEVE: Houston maybe. Dallas too.

MIRIAM: Gotcha.

STEVE: Where are you from?

MIRIAM: There are Jews everywhere. Can we change
the subject?

STEVE: Did you study this stuff? In college or something?

MIRIAM: Or something. Yeah.

STEVE: Yeah. *(Beat)* I took a religion class. I mean, it was a long time ago. In college.

MIRIAM: There you go.

STEVE: That thing you said about losing the Middleman. Luther said that. He was all about that. We studied Luther. In that class I took.

MIRIAM: Exactly. A lot of them said it.

STEVE: What's up with your cousin?

MIRIAM: Did I mention him?

STEVE: You did.

MIRIAM: He protects me from bad choices in love.

STEVE: Bad choices?

MIRIAM: Oh. Not you. I've made other bad choices.

STEVE: That's cool that you're Jewish.

MIRIAM: I don't know what you mean by that. But, sure.

Two

(Lights up on JUSTIN *and* TANGEE. TANGEE *is his girlfriend. She is a very young mom. She is in her early twenties but acts older, has a four year old daughter. Is not Jewish. Smiles a lot. Strong willed. Like a bull. And a flight attendant, too.)*

TANGEE: Glad I got the babysitter.

JUSTIN: The one Evelyn likes.

TANGEE: Evelyn loves her. She's a good girl, too.

JUSTIN: Have you heard from her dad?

TANGEE: The Fuckhead?

JUSTIN: Yeah. Him.

TANGEE: No.

JUSTIN: You might soon.

TANGEE: He's a fuckhead. Tell me about your day.

JUSTIN: It was good.

TANGEE: What'd you do?

JUSTIN: Um. You know. Worked. You know. Just worked. Music. Soundtrack. Can you guess what it was?

TANGEE: Are you trying to train me to be psychic like you?

JUSTIN: No. I like you the way you are.

TANGEE: Good. Because I don't know what you listened to while you were working.

(JUSTIN *shows* TANGEE *a C D case.*)

TANGEE: Okay. I never would have guessed that. *(Beat)* Sometimes you look at me like you're coming back from somewhere far away and you come back and recognize my face, and I like that.

JUSTIN: I'm not far away.

TANGEE: Sure you are. But I like that.

(Perhaps as they kiss)

TANGEE: They called from daycare. Evelyn wouldn't eat again.

JUSTIN: She misses her dad.

TANGEE: I love how you can just work from home. Don't you love that?

JUSTIN: Sure.

TANGEE: It's the greatest thing about this age. The age of technology.

JUSTIN: Information.

TANGEE: Excuse me?

JUSTIN: The age of information.

TANGEE: I thought that was the last age.

JUSTIN: Well. They still call it the age of information.

TANGEE: That's dumb.

JUSTIN: It's still information.

TANGEE: Shouldn't it have a new name? It's a new age.

JUSTIN: Well. No. It's still information. It's digital, but it's still information.

TANGEE: But that's dumb. It's a new century. We can't be in the same age. I want it to have a new name. And you know what I mean anyhow. About you working from home. Working from home is great. You can telecommute. I wish I could telecommute.

JUSTIN: Hard in retail.

TANGEE: I get other benefits. I get people.

JUSTIN: I don't get people.

TANGEE: You get me.

JUSTIN: That's a benefit.

TANGEE: You're good.

JUSTIN: I'm not.

TANGEE: You are though.

JUSTIN: I should tell you. My cousin's coming.

TANGEE: The crazy stripper?

JUSTIN: No. The other one.

TANGEE: Oh. With the truck?

JUSTIN: Yes. Her.

TANGEE: Oh. When?

JUSTIN: I'm not sure.

TANGEE: Will she stay long?

JUSTIN: I don't really know.

TANGEE: She used to live here.

JUSTIN: Yes. This is her house.

TANGEE: Did she call?

JUSTIN: Not exactly. I just have that feeling. You know. How I get that. It's in my hands.

TANGEE: Really?

JUSTIN: How was your day?

TANGEE: You get that a lot don't you? Those feelings?

JUSTIN: It's not a big deal.

TANGEE: It is a big deal.

JUSTIN: I won't tell you.

TANGEE: No. I like that you tell me.

JUSTIN: Right. You like hearing the weird things from the freak.

TANGEE: No. That's not it—

JUSTIN: Sure it is.

TANGEE: No. First of all, you don't tell me hardly anything let alone anything weird. And you're not a freak. You're kind of cute.

JUSTIN: Uh-huh. So she might show up. My cousin.

TANGEE: With the truck.

JUSTIN: Yes. And things happen when she's around. Freak things.

(SOPHY *addresses the audience.*)

SOPHY: Welcome Ye of the Congregation of the Broken Hearted. Welcome Motherless Children. Welcome you who wrestle with Angels. I used to wrestle with angels too. But not anymore.

I, Mistress Sophy, am the Spiritual Leader of the Congregation of the Broken Hearted, Musical Director of the Chorus of Falling Angels. Usher of the coming times, the world that is to come, constantly constantly constantly coming..... I know about constantly coming. And I bet you'd like to, huh? Want me to share? Because for a limited time only, for a drink and a good meal, for fifty bucks, maybe a hundred (*Cause rates are going up*) I'll tell you what I see and what I know. I'll look into your soul and tell you what I pick up. Want that? Fifty bucks to look at your soul, a hundred and I'll throw in a blowjob. No, I'm just kidding. I don't do that anymore.

Hey, I could be Elijah for all you know. Capitalism makes everyone a whore.

Maybe just maybe... I'm gonna tell you some secrets. For getting found. Cause getting lost is a thing of the past. And now we're all getting found.

Four

STEVE: You said your mom died?

MIRIAM: Last year.

STEVE: I'm sorry.

MIRIAM: It's not your fault.

STEVE: I know.

MIRIAM: I just hate when people say that. It's like—

STEVE: They just don't know what to say, that's all.

MIRIAM: No. It's like they have to say something and there's this thing that they say because that's what everyone says and it doesn't mean anything—it makes me mad.

STEVE: A lot of things make you mad.

MIRIAM: Yeah. So?

STEVE: So nothing. I'm just saying, a lot of things make you mad.

MIRIAM: I guess they do. *(She smiles; new topic.)* I'm an empath. Know what that means, Steve?

STEVE: No.

MIRIAM: It means I can feel what you're feeling.

STEVE: Is that why you're such a bitch right now?

MIRIAM: It is. Kind of.

STEVE: What am I feeling?

MIRIAM: Proud of yourself. For calling me a bitch. You like it that I didn't get offended. And you feel sort of guilty for asking about my mom. You hope I don't get sentimental because you hate watching women cry. And—oh—excitement— You're wondering if we'll have sex again.

STEVE: Will we?

MIRIAM: I don't know. You want to?

STEVE: I don't know.

MIRIAM: Yeah. We'll see.

STEVE: Your mom—*(Catches himself saying "I'm sorry" and stops)* It's rough.

MIRIAM: *(She shrugs)* Whatever. People die. People die all the time. It's a big part of life.

(SOPHY takes the narration—breaking into the storytelling—hijacking the audience away from her cousin.)

SOPHY: I've been a lot of people. Just in this one life.

Sophy—Birth through sixteen. Sophia means wisdom.

Star—sixteen, high school, unwashed hair, trying not to come home, trying so hard, hanging out, hanging out, hanging out, call me Star, yeah cause that's my name—

Satya—means truth in Sanskrit. Did you know I once danced with a group of Hare Krishnas and went home with them to pray and they told me I could be Satya, I could be truth, and so when I am dancing I am truth. (Even when I'm lying, I'm truth.)

Chaya—My rabbi gave me that name. And I went back and forth for a while, Sophy and Chaya, til Israel. But when I came back from Israel, I needed to be Star again cause I needed the money. Star makes money. And then, my Rabbi appeared again. He found me when I was about to lose my soul all over again, and this time, he called me Found. He called me that, and I was. Found.

Can I bum a cigarette?

MIRIAM: *(To* STEVE*)* Can I bum a cigarette?

(They both take cigarettes from STEVE, *who sees only* MIRIAM; *and their lines can overlap here.)*

SOPHY: Thanks, Baby. You're nice.

(From this point on SOPHY *can be integrated and overlapping with the other two.)*

MIRIAM: Thanks. You're nice.

*(*MIRIAM *and* STEVE *drive.)*

MIRIAM: I met this old guy outside the Safeway—when I lived in California—

SOPHY: I meet people all the time.

MIRIAM: He was maybe fifty, and he used to just hang out in the parking lot, and he had a theory about the

way the universe is put together. He said "It's all
colors, see—there are the reds and the greens. And
all of life, all the visuals, (he could see energy), it all
breaks down to either one or the other as a dominant
trait". He could see, visually, these two base colors
and their ratios in all the things of the material world.
He was in that parking lot just about every night. And
sometimes I'd go and buy him coffee and hang out. He
was my favorite kind of stranger.

STEVE: The kind you talk to.

MIRIAM: The kind that gets it.

SOPHY: The prophet kind.

MIRIAM: —who tells you things you need to know.

SOPHY: Do you like the Doors? Because I fucking *love*
the Doors. A lot of those songs were for me. I mean,
I wasn't alive yet, but on a cosmic level—they're for
me. My husband was a musician. Oh, I was married
once. In Israel. But lets not talk about it. Lets talk about
wandering prophets and holy strippers and glee. Lets
talk about glee. And the beautiful Doors. And all the
doorways I'm in and out of all time. Cause right now
I'm in the in-between, but pretty soon, I'll be moving
all the way across. To whatever it is that meets us,
greets us, refashions and lets us loose.

STEVE: You're that kind of stranger.

MIRIAM: I know.

STEVE: The kind that gets it.

MIRIAM: I've been told.

STEVE: I could be that kind of stranger too.

SOPHY: Yes. You could.

MIRIAM: Yes. You could.

STEVE: Yes. I could.

MIRIAM: In our religion, we call it Elijah. He's a wandering prophet, and anyone could be him, anyone. We're supposed to welcome him.

STEVE: You sure did that.

MIRIAM: I guess I did.

STEVE: I could know things for you.

MIRIAM: Like what?

STEVE: You're scared of your family. You're running.

MIRIAM: Don't you think it's way too easy to tell a wild thing that they're running?

STEVE: I don't know. I'm running too. That's how I can see it in you.

MIRIAM: I guess so.

STEVE: And now we go our separate ways?

MIRIAM: Yes. Now we go our separate ways.

STEVE: Well. We've got a few miles left. Til Akron.

(MIRIAM *and* STEVE *drive.*)

SOPHY: Sometimes they blur into one. My names. Who I've been. Who I am. Sometimes it's like becoming a new person and sometimes it's more like running from an old one. Sophy, the old one, talks too much and can't contain herself. I don't want to talk anymore. I want to stop bleeding on the table and staining all your furniture. I don't want to talk anymore, or leave stains. I never learned containment.

What's your name? I may have the gift, but it's not like a circus thing in a tent. I can't guess your name. But I can tell you where you're hurt and what you need. And I might be what you need. I really just might. Want me to be what you need?

Five

(MIRIAM *drops* STEVE *in Akron.*)

MIRIAM: So this is it. Akron.

STEVE: Should I say we'll be in touch?

MIRIAM: Not unless you want to.

STEVE: Okay. I won't.

MIRIAM: Thanks for the company though. It was nice.

STEVE: Thank you. For being that kind of stranger.

(MIRIAM *and* STEVE *kiss.*)

STEVE: You taste sweet.

MIRIAM: I wish I were. Sweet.

STEVE: Taste okay to me. Good luck with your family.

MIRIAM: Thank you. *(She knows she will need it)*

Six

TANGEE: You said something about love.

JUSTIN: What did I say?

TANGEE: You know.

JUSTIN: No. What did I say?

TANGEE: I cried when you said it. (Inside. I mean, I cried inside. Not so you could tell.) My ex would never have said something like that. He was a fuckhead. But you said it. And it reminded me of this guy I used to know, he was my roommate's boyfriend before I married the Fuckhead, and he used to say that when love comes, well, something about sticking out your chin. Like you just have to stick out your chin. And I was thinking about that after you said what you said.

JUSTIN: What did I say?

TANGEE: That you'd follow love. That if someone came along who altered your idea of love, you'd say yes, you'd go. And I cried when you said it (inside) because I wanted it to be me. That you'd say yes to. I want it to be me.

JUSTIN: It's not a person. I wasn't talking about a person. I'd be saying "yes" to love. Not a person.

TANGEE: I know. But I want it to be me.

JUSTIN: But it's just not a person. You say yes to Love itself, not a person.

TANGEE: Sure. I know that. *(Beat)* Evelyn likes you.

JUSTIN: She misses her dad.

TANGEE: She loves you; I love you. *(In a rush)* It's okay. You don't have to say it back. I know you don't like saying it. It's okay. I just needed to tell you. Okay, so that was a nice moment. Lets go out. Do you want to go out?

JUSTIN: I don't mind saying it.

TANGEE: No. It's fine. I know you don't like saying it, but I just need you to know—I am not a casual person, and— (Evelyn doesn't miss her dad; she doesn't know her dad) —

JUSTIN: I'm not a casual person.

TANGEE: Am I someone you could love?

JUSTIN: We're just getting to know each other.

TANGEE: So am I someone you could love?

JUSTIN: It's early. We're just starting to get to know each other—

TANGEE: No. If you were in love with me, you'd know.

JUSTIN: I don't think about things that way.

TANGEE: I do. And you would.

JUSTIN: It's early.

TANGEE: Sure. But, for the record, I am not a casual person. I don't just do this. What we're doing. I have to like someone. And I think about things. I have a child. I have to think, for my child, about things that have substance.

JUSTIN: I'm not a casual person.

TANGEE: And I just want you to know, if we ever got serious, I would be willing to convert. If that's an issue for you. Because it isn't for me.

JUSTIN: Convert to what?

TANGEE: Judaism.

JUSTIN: You'd convert to Judaism.

TANGEE: Yes. I don't mind. I don't have a personal relationship with Jesus or anything.

JUSTIN: I see.

TANGEE: And I love all the food. What we had at the holiday. I could make that. What's the fish called again?

JUSTIN: Gefilte.

TANGEE: Right. I could make that.

JUSTIN: I don't really like gefilte fish.

TANGEE: Yes, but I'm just saying. I could make it.

JUSTIN: Well. I appreciate that you would—but, I don't think about things that way. And... it's not something I'm overtly looking for—a Jewess. It's not exactly one of the things I'm—

(This is interrupted by the arrival of MIRIAM. *Who still has keys.)*

MIRIAM: Well, welcome me home. *(Noticing* TANGEE*)* Oh. Hi there.

(TANGEE jumps up.)

TANGEE: I'm Tangee. Justin's girlfriend. Friend.

JUSTIN: I knew you were coming.

MIRIAM: Of course you did.

Seven

SOPHY: A sex worker exchanges sex or sexual energy or a sexual performance or images for money. Call girls, exotic dancers, porn models, phone workers and professional dominitrixes are all sex workers. The sex industry refers to the community or non-community of places and ways in which sex workers do their jobs. Escort services, adult film makers, actors and distributors are all examples of the sex industry. *(She removes her outer layer to reveal "stripper garb")*The kind of work I did was very supportive of my personality structure. I was a bad waitress. I hate desks. Social work really ripped me up. You can't do that and be empathic. It messes you up. I'm the type to bleed for money and feed the hungry—they're just hungry. And for the record, I have never had actual intercourse for money. I did other things.

In the old days, sex workers were emmissaries and carriers. We carried the word and made it flesh. We were vessels. Priestesses. I remember that. Dancing on the steps of the temple and how you paid us to come into the Word itself. To touch the Divine through our bodies. Learning mouth to mouth and face to face.

So if I take your mouth to my face, we are exchanging ancient knowledge. Information. Some of it has to be exchanged this way, without words. And it all runs together, the information and the fluids. Liquid light. An exchange of knowledge.

Want to exchange some knowledge?

Eight

MIRIAM: I can't believe you live here. In my old house.

TANGEE: He's been working on it. Since your mom.
I mean, in the last year. He's been doing all these
renovations. Those shelves.

MIRIAM: They're nice.

JUSTIN: I like living here. Don't look at me like that.

TANGEE: I helped. With the shelves. Well, I didn't
help that much. But I painted some. Aren't they great
looking? Aren't they?

MIRIAM: Great-looking. What do you do again,
Tammy?

TANGEE: Tangee. It's short for Angela.

MIRIAM: Is it?

TANGEE: Yes. It is. I work in retail.

MIRIAM: Do you?

JUSTIN: She's a manager.

MIRIAM: Of course she is.

JUSTIN: You want to eat? Are you hungry? There's a
place, it's new, you'd like it—

MIRIAM: Not now. I'm getting to know Tammy.

TANGEE: Tangee. He said you were in Mexico. I'd love
to go to Mexico. I had some girlfriends who went to
Cancun, it was a long time ago, and we were—

MIRIAM: How long have you two been...?

JUSTIN: Four months.

MIRIAM: That's a long time.

TANGEE: No, it's actually very early. We don't know if
we're going to get serious. It's really very early.

MIRIAM: I see.

JUSTIN: We met at her store.

MIRIAM: You said.

TANGEE: He was trying on shirts.

MIRIAM: Sure he was. I bet he looked great in those shirts. *(To* JUSTIN*)* They're not really you.

TANGEE: Oh they're great shirts.

JUSTIN: Tell us about your trip. Trips. I like the shirts. I wear them.

MIRIAM: My trips were good. Not much to tell. Some spooky stuff but I guess you wouldn't like that too much, would you?

TANGEE: Spooky stuff? Like ghosts? Evelyn, that's my daughter, she's going to be a ghost for—

MIRIAM: Halloween?

JUSTIN: Lets hear about your trip. Mexico City. Then—

MIRIAM: Further south. I just kept going. *(To* TANGEE*)* I had always wanted to just keep going. But there was always some reason to come back. This time, I just went—there was nothing to come back for.

JUSTIN: That's not true.

MIRIAM: What do you mean by that?

JUSTIN: I just mean—there wasn't nothing to come back for.

MIRIAM: What was there to come back for?

TANGEE: Do you want something? Should I put water on? For tea? Do you want tea? Or a drink? We have, Justin has—

MIRIAM: No. I want to hear more about what there was to come back for.

TANGEE: I like to travel. I do. I've been to, well, Los Angeles. We took a tour of the Disney studios. And saw the Hollywood sign. I've been to the Grand Canyon. My ex the Fuckhead had family around there. We lived in Dallas very briefly. I visited Houston once or twice. They have very good museums in Houston. My daughter, I try to take her to museums. I just think children need to be around art as much as they can.

JUSTIN: You look too hard.

MIRIAM: I missed you. What do you think I look "too hard" for?

TANGEE: He knew you were coming today. He had this, um you know he just knew. Feeling.

JUSTIN: What was it you were doing down there again?

MIRIAM: Um, travelling?

JUSTIN: Right. That.

MIRIAM: I learn through travel. I pick things up, meet people.

JUSTIN: I know.

MIRIAM: They're strangers, and then they're not.

JUSTIN: I know.

MIRIAM: I take them places. I take them in, these pieces of them, then I go to the next place.

JUSTIN: So you're the Lone Ranger.

MIRIAM: Shut up.

JUSTIN: (To TANGEE) Are you hungry? I'm getting hungry.

MIRIAM: My God, In Mexico it's all about dairy products. They're everywhere. You'd think rice and beans, and sure, rice and beans but cooked with pork and served with dairy products. Cream and milk and cheese. You have to be like "Sin crema" all the time.

Otherwise lots of "crema" on everything. Everything.
And I"m like SIN CREMA—NO CREAM, NO
CREAM—and they're like "why?"

TANGEE: Why?

MIRIAM: I ate meat. I had to. For grounding. I was
doing so much work with my hands and body. And
learning about energy and how it moves. Doing all this
stuff—

TANGEE: Why?

MIRIAM: Why was I doing stuff?

TANGEE: No, the food. Why are they like "why" when
you say "no cream"?

JUSTIN: I'd love it.

MIRIAM: You would love it. *(To* TANGEE*)* It's a poor
country. They can't understand why an American,
from a rich country, would, you know, choose not to
eat meat or cream.

JUSTIN: No wonder you look so good.

MIRIAM: That's not it. I had really great sex with this
guy I picked up in Texas.

TANGEE: I like to eat turkey. Lean turkey breast. I read
somewhere, in a health magazine, that lean turkey
breast— *(She realizes no one is listening to her.)* Justin
is doing really well. With his work here. He totally
survived the dot-com crash.

JUSTIN: Well, what I do isn't exactly part of—

MIRIAM: That's why I look good.

JUSTIN: Of course.

MIRIAM: I wanted to stay. Down there. In Mexico.

TANGEE: Why didn't you?

MIRIAM: *(To* JUSTIN*)* Somebody called me back.

(Innocently, she reaches to scratch her skin...the start of an itch)

Nine

SOPHY: Our Grandma, Lena, did not believe in religion. Judaism had nothing for her. She raised rule-less, Godless children, three of them, and they raised us. But the Jewish soul longs so much for God, we can't be satisfied with a non-Jewish path. And they're running around, these assimilated American Jews, with no idea, none, that what they're hungry for is what they're running from. And it can't be erased, the Jewish longing for God, Hashem. Like a bride for her bridegroom. And Lena—who didn't "believe"—still said the blessings every Friday night—in Hebrew, she lit candles and said them, with her hands covering her face and a napkin on her head.

She'd say "I wish for you all the things,". Only the things never turn out quite the way our grandmas wish them, do they?

Ten

TANGEE: *(Also to the audience)* There are ski people and there are lodge people. I'm a lodge person. I don't like to get wet. Or cold. But I am really good at keeping things moving at home in the lodge. I'm really good at making sure there is hot chocolate and a fire all ready when you come in to get warm. I like the fire in the lodge. I like the wood panelling. I look really cute in ski sweaters. But I'm not about the actual skiing. I mean, come on. Look at me. I am all about Lodge.

She is all about skiiing. Not only that. She is all about daring skiiing. I mean, when she gets back to the lodge she tells all the men all these stories about the risks she took out on the slopes, skiiing, she doesn't even wear the right gear, she just like goes up there and has to tell everyone how she was daring and met animals or whatever—and everyone has to listen because there's no T V in the lodge, just me and drinks and the fire

I don't care to hear about all her stories. I wish she'd just go back where she came from and leave the lodge to those of us who know what it is for.

Eleven

(MIRIAM *and* JUSTIN *alone, after* TANGEE's *gone home.*)

MIRIAM: What's with the name? She sounds like a Starburst fruit chew.

JUSTIN: Tangee. Like Tangiers.

MIRIAM: She is hardly Tangiers. She's more Tulsa.

JUSTIN: Tangible. Able to be known. Able to be seen.

MIRIAM: Can you lose her somewhere?

JUSTIN: I don't want to lose her.

MIRIAM: I think you could do better.

JUSTIN: I don't think we should talk about this.

MIRIAM: You brought it up.

JUSTIN: No. I just said—

MIRIAM: Would you come with me? Next time?

JUSTIN: Tangible is a fine quality to have. It is not always necessary to be mysterious and ethereal.

MIRIAM: That's not what I'm saying. I'm saying—

JUSTIN: Where is it you want to go?

MIRIAM: Anywhere. I want to go anywhere.

JUSTIN: Now? You want to go now?

MIRIAM: I don't know. I just got here. Maybe not now. But soon. I want to go soon. I met these guys in Mexico who told me about *(This place outside Monterey)*—

JUSTIN: No.

MIRIAM: Why?

JUSTIN: I have stuff here —

MIRIAM: Exactly. Lose the stuff.

JUSTIN: It's not her.

MIRIAM: Sure.

JUSTIN: I have a business.

MIRIAM: Right.

JUSTIN: Which I like. Which is creative. Not all attachment is bad.

MIRIAM: Sure.

JUSTIN: I have stuff to figure out.

MIRIAM: And where are you going to do that? In your head?

JUSTIN: You just got home. Stop picking fights.

MIRIAM: I am not picking fights.

JUSTIN: I'm thinking of building a sun porch. On the side of the house. What do you think of that?

MIRIAM: Trying to encapsulate our entire sense of family into this one physical structure is bad. And I can't help picking fights, I am an incendiary person.

JUSTIN: Look. I have to live somewhere. And who says it's bad?

MIRIAM: But it shouldn't have to be physical. Our sense of home.

JUSTIN: Not everyone wants to live in a truck.

MIRIAM: Says everyone. Everyone says that about sense of home.

JUSTIN: In other cultures, people stay in the family home and—

MIRIAM: I don't like her for you.

JUSTIN: Yes. You said.

MIRIAM: She's not special.

JUSTIN: You said that too.

MIRIAM: Well, I'm saying it again.

JUSTIN: I like her. I learn things. It's good.

MIRIAM: You "learn things"? What could you possibly—

JUSTIN: Don't. I'm getting stuff about Sophy. In my hands. Are you?

MIRIAM: No.

JUSTIN: You're not?

(MIRIAM *shrugs.*)

JUSTIN: She wakes me up. She's screaming in the middle of the night.

MIRIAM: She's a pain in the ass. She always was.

JUSTIN: She's screaming.

MIRIAM: I don't get anything.

JUSTIN: *(Calling her bluff)* Liar.

(MIRIAM *says nothing.*)

JUSTIN: I think that's why you came home.

MIRIAM: Because she's screaming?

JUSTIN: Because she's calling us.

(SOPHY *calls a time-out*)

SOPHY: Oh, I just love when they get dramatic.

In the house with the seventy elders little girls are put to bed at the right time. No one fights and no one complains. Furniture stays put. Glassware doesn't break. Nothing gets hurled across the room and there are no late night outbursts. In the house with the seventy elders everyone knows his place. Or hers. It is always time for milk and cookies and the Elders are God's emmisaries and they are watching over you. And me. They are watching over little girls who get hurt in the night. And no one hurts these little girls or touches them or puts cigarettes out on their arms and little girls live free and no one touches them ever.

My rabbi showed me a world with rules. No one touches anyone except under the contract called marriage. And dancing is like that too. There are rules and a large man enforcing them. You can't touch me. I touch you. You do not touch back. Usually I'm behind glass.

Okay. Lets go back to them—being dramatic.

(*And, we are sent back to* MIRIAM *and* JUSTIN, *still fighting: they fight like siblings.*)

MIRIAM: —all I'm saying is dump her. That's all I'm saying.

JUSTIN: —this "we're special" bullshit is bullshit.

MIRIAM: I know you.

JUSTIN: So?

MIRIAM: You're like me. Don't you get it? We're alike.

JUSTIN: Alike does not mean undifferentiated.

MIRIAM: You don't get it. You don't get it. I can't even talk to you because you won't even get it.

JUSTIN: What is it you think I don't get?

MIRIAM: What I see in you.

JUSTIN: Which is?

MIRIAM: Huge. Holy and huge.

JUSTIN: I don't want to talk about this.

MIRIAM: You can't just waste yourself here, in my old house -

JUSTIN: I feel you all the time. All the time. When you're gone. I know where you are, what you're doing and feeling—It's not just Sophy. You scream too.

MIRIAM: So come with me. Okay, at least come with me *now*. Tonight. We'll get french fries and a bottle of cheap wine—you like that, right? And sit in the tree and watch things like we used to.

JUSTIN: I'm tired.

MIRIAM: So we'll get coffee.

JUSTIN: I don't feel like it.

MIRIAM: When will you feel like it?

JUSTIN: I don't know.

Twelve

SOPHY: This is the best part. How I Met Him.

Okay, so to start with, here's me, eighteen, tripping, barefoot, in college, at the Student Union, I was always surprised that no one seemed to notice, I mean, I still got good grades and—so, here's me, barefoot and dancing and high, stealing muffins from the cafeteria—I finally got out of the house, that one I grew up in, but for what? I mean, I thought I'd leave home and this whole shining life would be there waiting for me, and The Shining Life would say "Thank you for your great courage, for surviving that mess of

a family. Thank You—for getting out. No one ever
believed you and no one ever stopped the bad things
from happening and no one heard you scream, but
Good Girl Good Girl Good GOOD GOOD GOOD how
you got yourself out. We, your Shining Life Guardian
Angels, have been waiting for you. Here's your good
girl new life, waiting." Only it wasn't like that at all.
Nobody took me in their arms. And nothing was
waiting. And my mother still called me in the middle
of the night drunk and both of them, my parents, even
expected me to come home on vacations and act like a
perfect, normal suburban girl only I'd get thrown out if
I showed up discernably high or if they found anything
on me, so okay, I got thrown out a lot. I mean, a lot. Til
I left forever.

And then, I met them, my rabbi and his wife.
Someone brought me, and there I was. At the Student
Union. Union of students. In Union. Barefoot and high.
With a group of Jews. I don't remember too much else
about it. But I think it saved my life. The union of the
students, and him. I dropped out of school and studied
and gathered and celebrated and ate and I met that
musician and we moved to Israel, made aliyat, and
then I left his ratty ass and came back again, single,
broke and disowned. But never happier.

And even when I danced, for money, even when I left
the community, or went back, or was poor and making
big mistakes, I made mistakes—I always had Hashem.
I was never lost.

The world makes you think there's something in
between YOU and where your soul comes from. But
what if there isn't? What if there isn't?

Come on, Sweet One. Ye of Little Faith. Come on,
come on, come on, come on...

(Jim Morrison Come on Touch me Baby *plays loudly.
There may be a sound/light collage here. something which*

indicates that SOPHY's *monologue and* MIRIAM's *bad dream are coinciding.* SOPHY *dances in bliss and rapture, calling the others to her.)*

Thirteen

(JUSTIN *is working.* MIRIAM *is just getting up. She's in her underwear, or his—and a ripped t-shirt. She attempts to make coffee. He's nearby. On a laptop, maybe.* MIRIAM *is itching, but still very very subtly, as if from dry skin.)*

MIRIAM: Okay, so I dreamed about her too.

JUSTIN: Yeah?

MIRIAM: She called me "Ye of Little Faith." It pissed me off.

JUSTIN: Sophy? Piss you off? Really?

MIRIAM: Shut up.

JUSTIN: Sure.

MIRIAM: Dogmatism runs in our family. We are all dogmatic.

JUSTIN: I am not dogmatic.

MIRIAM: Sure you are. You just don't tell anyone what you're thinking.

JUSTIN: Okay.

MIRIAM: You got any espresso?

JUSTIN: No.

MIRIAM: Okay.

JUSTIN: There's a place nearby—

MIRIAM: No.

JUSTIN: There's a store too. They have—

MIRIAM: Yeah. Maybe that. I could go pick up some really nice espresso. I don't drink this instant crap.

JUSTIN: I see that.

MIRIAM: Do you?

JUSTIN: I don't mind it.

MIRIAM: That's fucked.

JUSTIN: Maybe.

MIRIAM: I saw an angel.

JUSTIN: In the kitchen?

MIRIAM: In my dreams.

JUSTIN: What kind of angel?

MIRIAM: The kind that tells you things.

JUSTIN: What did it tell you?

MIRIAM: To go buy espresso.

JUSTIN: I see.

MIRIAM: You might be right. About Sophy. I think you could be right.

JUSTIN: I'm usually right.

MIRIAM: But I don't want to see her. I don't want to get involved in any more dramatic, draining, overwhelming—

JUSTIN: Too bad.
It's family.

(And now, the three enter "psychic half time" —a clear and direct state in which they can access one another. The three come together. It is as if JUSTIN and MIRIAM's connection activates the gift and calls SOPHY to them.)

MIRIAM: It's his idea. I said you were fine.

JUSTIN: We're getting dreams—

MIRIAM: He is. He's worried.

JUSTIN: I'm not worried. Do you want us to find you?

SOPHY: I'm fine.

MIRIAM: *(To* JUSTIN*)* See? She's fine. Good.

SOPHY: I'm more than fine.

JUSTIN: Good.

SOPHY: I'm great.

MIRIAM: Great.

SOPHY: Why wouldn't I be?

JUSTIN: Well—

MIRIAM: Oh lots of reasons. That heroin-using boyfriend who hit you—

SOPHY:—Once. He hit me once.

MIRIAM: Right. Telephone jobs, stripping—

SOPHY: Dancing

MIRIAM: Bad memories, bad gin, the past, your father, your mother—

JUSTIN: We just want to make sure you're okay.

SOPHY: Okay. I'm okay.

JUSTIN: We just wanted to make sure. Can you come home for a while?

SOPHY: I"m really busy.

MIRIAM: She's busy.

SOPHY: I'm busy with Jim Morrison.

JUSTIN: Jim Morrison?

SOPHY: He's my soulmate. We have a date to meet.

MIRIAM: A date to meet where?

SOPHY: In the aftertime. The swing between worlds.

JUSTIN: I see.

SOPHY: Yes. So I'm really busy getting ready. And I'm having this amazing love affair with Hashem. God. I'm writing love letters all the time. To Him. And He answers back too. All the time in all sorts of ways. It's an everlasting love with an everliving God.

MIRIAM: See. She's fine.

JUSTIN: Honey. Can you come home?

SOPHY: No. I told you. I'm so busy.

MIRIAM: Busy and happy and fine—

SOPHY: Free. Or I will be real soon. Free.

JUSTIN: What does that mean?

(Beat; SOPHY doesn't answer.)

JUSTIN: Can you tell us where you are?

SOPHY: No. I like it better when you have to find me.

(Lights out)

Fourteen

(MIRIAM and JUSTIN get ready to go, packing up the truck , ready for travel. TANGEE tries to help JUSTIN.)

MIRIAM: We have to go now. Bye, Tammy. We're looking for our crazy stripper cousin and it might take a really long time. Who even knows where we'll end up. We could just be gone forever.

TANGEE: Tangee.

MIRIAM: What?

TANGEE: Tangee. It's short for Angela. That's my name.

MIRIAM: Oh. Sorry. (To JUSTIN) I'll wait in the truck. (She exits.)

JUSTIN: I won't be gone long.

TANGEE: Okay.

JUSTIN: I'm coming back.

TANGEE: Sure.

JUSTIN: I'm coming back.

TANGEE: It's fine. It's too early to have to make promises.

JUSTIN: What are you talking about?

TANGEE: Maybe you'll meet someone. More like you. Out there. You never know.

JUSTIN: My cousin is in trouble.

TANGEE: Sure. I'm just saying. Maybe you'll meet someone. You never know.

JUSTIN: I'm not going to meet anyone. I'm looking for my cousin. She's in trouble.

TANGEE: No, you don't know that. You just get these feelings, and then you think you know things, but, I mean, you just get these feelings. And I know that she doesn't like me, your cousin with the truck, I know that. I may not be psychic like all of you, but I know she doesn't like me, and you all probably just wish I'd go away—And how do you know what you're gonna do? What if you end up in Mexico?

JUSTIN: I'm not going to Mexico. I speak three words of Spanish and two of them are "sin crema"—I am coming back.

TANGEE: You are?

JUSTIN: Yes. I am. *(He kisses* TANGEE *on the forehead or the very top of her head, as if she's a child.)* Love you.

*(*JUSTIN *exits, following* MIRIAM. TANGEE *is alone on stage.)*

TANGEE: You left out the "I".

Fifteen

(A young revisionist RABBI *addresses the audience.)*

RABBI: The *Sh'ma* is the central prayer of Jewish practice. *Sh'ma Yisrael Adonai Elohenu Adonai Echad.* It is most commonly translated, in English, as "Hear, O Israel, The Lord our God, the Lord is One." However, if look at each of the words that make up the prayer, we find that we might translate this very differently.

Sh'ma: Listen, open yourself, listen

Y'Israel: the name given to Jacob after he wrestled with God, or the angel as sometimes translated. So this might mean, You who wrestle with the truth

Adonai—the nameless, formless, boundless energy of God

Eloheinu—the contained and concealed name for God—so the boundless can be contained in this world

Adonai—the boundless again

Echad—One.

So—Listen, you who wrestle with truth and angels, the boundless nameless energy of Holiness is contained and concealed within this world, and this endless good is One, Unity, it emanates as One.

Sixteen

*(*TANGEE *goes to see the* RABBI.*)*

TANGEE: I"d like to learn to be Jewish.

RABBI: I see.

TANGEE: does it take a long time?

RABBI: To learn?

TANGEE: To convert.

RABBI: Well, you have to study.

TANGEE: I know. I'll study.

RABBI: And convert.

TANGEE: Sure.

RABBI: Why do you want to do this? Why do you want to be a Jew?

TANGEE: Stand by your Man?

RABBI: I see.

TANGEE: It's just that he's Jewish, and I want to have another baby before I'm thirty—and I'm only twenty-four now, but I like to think ahead, and I know that the mother has to be Jewish for the child to be Jewish, and I was thinking, he ran off with his cousin, and she drives this truck and there's something between them and it's—it makes me uncomfortable.

RABBI: His cousin?

TANGEE: She drives a truck.

RABBI: I see.

TANGEE: What do you think I should do?

Seventeen

(JUSTIN *and* MIRIAM *in her truck. She drives. He navigates.* SOPHY *is this scene as a physical presence. Now that they're moving closer, she is with them all the time.*)

JUSTIN: She used to call. At strange hours. Just to talk. Then she stopped. She even stopped inviting me to those functions.

MIRIAM: Holidays?

JUSTIN: Shabbos dinner mostly. She'd call from the city inviting me, and it always included staying over for Shabbos dinner.

MIRIAM: Oh. I wouldn't—

JUSTIN: I went once. It was depressing. They kept introducing me to—

MIRIAM: This girl is not your equal. You know that.

JUSTIN: I don't really want to talk about this. Your own lovers, besides being somewhat random, are—

MIRIAM: I know—

JUSTIN: Exactly.

MIRIAM: I make bad choices. I've been told I have a death wish in love.

JUSTIN: Great.

MIRIAM: You look out for me. I just want to—

JUSTIN: I don't have a death wish. In love.

MIRIAM: Boredom and death are the same thing.

JUSTIN: I don't have a boredom wish.

MIRIAM: Okay.

JUSTIN: Lets just focus on Sophy.

SOPHY: ...pure, clean and beautiful...we are pure, clean and beautiful.... You fed me and found me. You broke me til I broke—

JUSTIN: She stopped calling a few weeks ago.

SOPHY: Someone is looking for me, but I am not a lost soul.

MIRIAM: She's lost. she's crazy.

SOPHY: I am not a lost soul.

JUSTIN: It isn't your fault.

SOPHY: The vessel has to be shattered.

MIRIAM: I didn't say it was.

SOPHY: Before it can be refashioned.

JUSTIN: I know. But I'm just saying.

SOPHY: to contain more of G-d. To seal up all the leaks, the places where power leaks out. The vessel has to be shattered before it can be rebuilt to contain the word. and keep it there, contained and not leaking.

(SOPHY *reaches out to* MIRIAM, *almost touching her or becoming close in some way that makes her pull away—*)

MIRIAM: Don't.

JUSTIN: Don't what!?

MIRIAM: Don't say it's not my fault. Don't say you're sorry. Don't say you love me. Don't. (*She turns up the radio really loud.*)

Eighteen

TANGEE: Remember me?

RABBI: Of course I do. Stand by your man.

TANGEE: Right.

TANGEE: They're in Mexico.

RABBI: Mexico?

TANGEE: Well not Mexico. Who knows where they went. They have this crazy stripper cousin, and she's in some kind of trouble, but I think they're just running away together because she hates me so much—

RABBI: The stripper?

TANGEE: No. The other one. With the truck.

RABBI: Oh. The trucker.

(TANGEE *smiles.*)

TANGEE: Yes.

RABBI: Are you sure they're Jewish?

TANGEE: Absolutely.

RABBI: So what can I do for you?

TANGEE: Well. I want to learn more. Teach me. Not just about the religion. I want to—

RABBI: A reading list?

TANGEE: Sure. Lets start with a reading list.

Nineteen

(JUSTIN *and* MIRIAM *sit in a diner.* SOPHY *slides into the booth with them or sits in the booth right behind them. Or perhaps she's the waitress. In some way, however, she is present.)*

JUSTIN: Her shul. Haddassah. The Old Neighborhood. Then the bars.

MIRIAM: Whose old neighborhood?

JUSTIN: The old Jewish neighborhood.

MIRIAM: Oh.

JUSTIN: It's where everything is. The geography is precise.

MIRIAM: You know a lot about this.

JUSTIN: It interests me.

MIRIAM: Clearly.

JUSTIN: I was in touch with her. When you were away. I visited a few times—

MIRIAM: Do you go to strip clubs?

JUSTIN: Uh. I have. On occasion.

MIRIAM: What's up with them?

JUSTIN: In what sense?

MIRIAM: Are they sexy?

JUSTIN: Sure. Visually.

MIRIAM: I see.

JUSTIN: I mean except when I look too hard to see if any of the girls are my cousin. That just kills the visual. But they're—it's a very specific language of sexy. A visual shorthand. For sexy. Yeah, okay, I guess they're sexy.

MIRIAM: Did you know what was happening to Sophy when we were kids?

JUSTIN: I don't know.

MIRIAM: I did.

JUSTIN: I know.

MIRIAM: She used to come over. She and my mom were so close.

JUSTIN: Your mom could make anyone feel special.

MIRIAM: Yes. She could. She was a special person, my mother.

JUSTIN: And she smelled good. You knew things were going to be okay when she was around.

MIRIAM: And Sophy just took her over. Like she takes everything. And she couldn't have my mother, she was *my* mother—

JUSTIN: It wasn't your—

MIRIAM: I know.

JUSTIN: —fault.

MIRIAM: But it kind of was. I mean—it was. I knew what was happening to Sophy and I didn't do anything. I knew about her mother. And how Sophy was being—treated—and—my mom knew, but much much after I did. And my mom tried to help, but I didn't. I hated her. Even then. How can you hate someone who -?

JUSTIN: You were a kid.

MIRIAM: Hatred's hatred.

JUSTIN: Sibling rivalry.

MIRIAM: We weren't siblings. We were cousins.

JUSTIN: We acted like siblings.

MIRIAM: I don't think I've made any progress at all. On not hating her. All I had in the whole world was this one sweet-smelling—

JUSTIN: You had me. You have me.

MIRIAM: Yeah?

JUSTIN: Yeah.

JUSTIN: But I want to have you more.

Twenty

RABBI: —it's an infinitely practical religion. An embodied religion. A religion that encourages us to be in the world.

TANGEE: *(Taking notes)* "Encourages us to be...in the..."

RABBI: —not a transcendent religion.

TANGEE: "Not a transcend..."

RABBI: What we practice, Reform Judaism, is practical and user-friendly, family-based—

TANGEE: I have a daughter.

RABBI: This is the religion. Having a daughter.

TANGEE: Being in the world.

RABBI: We're not afraid of the world. It's where we partner God.

TANGEE: Sure.

RABBI: I would like to have a daughter. Someday.

TANGEE: Are you married?

RABBI: Not yet. I haven't met the right person. I would like to be. But I haven't met the right person.

TANGEE: I was married. Way too young. High school sweetheart.

RABBI: They say people shouldn't.. you know, until they know themselves.

TANGEE: We did not know ourselves.

RABBI: And this boyfriend?

TANGEE: Yeah, who knows if that'll last.

RABBI: No one knows.

TANGEE: I sure don't.

RABBI: Where's your family?

TANGEE: Far. Tell me more about being in the world.

RABBI: Well. It's not a preparation. For Heaven or Hell or Judgement. Everything we do here is an opportunity, an invitation, to live as God would have us live. To partner Him. And to bring His Will into Action. Into form. Everything we do counts.

TANGEE: Yes. I believe that.

Twenty-one

MIRIAM: We're looking for you.

SOPHY: I know.

MIRIAM: Are you okay?

SOPHY: I'm good.

MIRIAM: Well, that's good. Cause I fucking ache.

SOPHY: Oh. You should meet my rabbi.

(Taking us into flashback)

MIRIAM: No, thank you. I hate that shit.

SOPHY: I know you do.

MIRIAM: It's sexist. And restrictive. And it all got translated wrong.

SOPHY: Sure. But you're a Jew.

MIRIAM: Sure.

SOPHY: And it's a rich tradition.

MIRIAM: Whatever.

SOPHY: What do you even know about being Jewish? You don't know what being Jewish means.

MIRIAM: Sure I do. We went to Sunday school.

SOPHY: Oh yeah, and that was really informative.

MIRIAM: I studied the Kabbalah. On one of my trips. With mystics.

SOPHY: Don't you think it's interesting that so many young Jewish people feel they have to go outside the faith to find a spiritual path?

MIRIAM: The Kabbalah is not outside our faith.

SOPHY: Why aren't we looking within our own traditions?

MIRIAM: The Kabbalah is within our tradition—

SOPHY: Yeah, but all the hocus pocus isn't. The yoga and the Buddhist retreats and the New Age goddess books—

MIRIAM: It was a lunar calendar Sophy. That's all it was. And I was twenty. And you ran away with the Hare Krishnas when you were Satya—

SOPHY: I'm just saying. You can search all you like. But you have a Jewish soul.

MIRIAM: And that means what? Forget everything else?

SOPHY: Just talk to my rabbi.

MIRIAM: No thank you.

SOPHY: But why? Why are you so closed to—

(Frustrated, MIRIAM *cuts* SOPHY *off.)*

MIRIAM: Why do we have to be more "Jewish"? Why is it always about tribal identity. Can't we be of a larger world?

SOPHY: No. You're a Jew. You were chosen.

MIRIAM: But why can't we as Jews be of a larger world? And isn't everyone chosen?

SOPHY: No. We're chosen. And the world hates us for being Jews. And you might not "identify", but let me tell you, other people will "identify" for you, other people will call you Jew, Hebe, Kike, greedy, money-hungry, violent, or dirty; they'll tell you your people are taking over. Cockroaches. That's what they called us in Germany. So you go on with your nonsectarian spirituality and your lunar calendars and whatever, but you were born a Jew and you will die a Jew.

MIRIAM: I hate this. I just hate it. I have a soul. I have a big soul, a post-denominational, transpersonal, nonsectarian transreligion soul. Stop putting a label on things just because you need a label there.

SOPHY: You have a Jewish soul. Eventually you will come home.

*(*MIRIAM *starts scratching at her skin. Somewhere. It's subtle.)*

MIRIAM: I can't talk to you.

SOPHY: Because you don't like what I say.

MIRIAM: You're right. I don't. How did you get like this?

SOPHY: Like what? How did I get like what?

MIRIAM: First it was all those drugs, then this.
(Gesturing at SOPHY's *clothes)* And it's all the same hole
in you, the same place where you just want to be taken
over— Why do you want to be taken over like that?

SOPHY: Stop talking. Stop talking now.

MIRIAM: Why? Why do you leave like that? It's like
you're leaving—

SOPHY: *(Exploding)* Stop. Stop fucking talking now.
You don't understand, so don't talk. Just shut up about
things you should not be talking about.

*(*SOPHY *storms off as* JUSTIN *enters—he is present for that
last beat of the scene—)*

MIRIAM: The last time I saw Sophy. We argued. At first
it wasn't serious, and then it got serious. And she was
the one to leave.

(And now, JUSTIN *takes us to another flashback, his last
encounter with* SOPHY.)*

JUSTIN: The last time I saw her....

SOPHY: Sweet One.

JUSTIN: I'm sorry I didn't come Friday night.

SOPHY: I could introduce you to some really nice girls.

JUSTIN: No thank you.

SOPHY: Oh come on. Not strippers. Jewish girls. Nice
girls.

JUSTIN: Um. Thanks, no. I've started seeing someone.

SOPHY: Is she Jewish?

JUSTIN: No. But she's really nice.

SOPHY: Oh.

JUSTIN: She's got a daughter. She's great. And a great
mother. She's just a great mom. She's from Texas, and
then she moved up here and—

SOPHY: She's not Jewish.

JUSTIN: Right. But I like her.

SOPHY: Mmm-hmm. Do you feel like a Jew? I mean, do you have any understanding of your responsiblity as a Jew?

JUSTIN: I guess.

SOPHY: I know. You have no idea. We weren't raised well.

JUSTIN: Well. I was bar-mitzvah'd.

SOPHY: I remember.

JUSTIN: And I've been racially stereotyped. But do we have to find identity through persecution?

SOPHY: Maybe. Maybe we do.

JUSTIN: How are you? Are you—?

SOPHY: Oh. You know.

JUSTIN: No. I don't know.

SOPHY: Well. Trying to—not do the things I usually do to make money. But it's all okay. My Rabbi, he says I should get married again. He's setting me up. They call. These men. Widowers. I met one. He was fat. And kinda old, too. But they call. It's okay. My Rabbi says it's what I need.

JUSTIN: You're like thirty. You should be—I don't know if you should be dating fat old widowers. You could do anything you want—you have nothing holding you back—

SOPHY: Everyone is married. In my community, at least. You should get married.

JUSTIN: What about school? Could you go back to school?

SOPHY: Don't start. You got any ice cream?

JUSTIN: No. We could go out. Do you want to go out?

SOPHY: I can't believe you live here.

JUSTIN: Yes. I live her.

SOPHY: This place, it's Her House, it makes me think of—

JUSTIN: Me too.

SOPHY: She was the best person. My favorite person.

JUSTIN: Yeah.

SOPHY: You heard from your parents?

JUSTIN: My mom called. I don't know, a week ago? They're—they never say much, I think they're fine.

SOPHY: Yeah. They never had a chance, that whole generation, that whole generation was just not okay. Mine, I'm glad they're dead. I'm glad. They were sick people, my parents. *(Changing the subject)* I dream about Miriam. Do you?

(JUSTIN nods.)

SOPHY: She's running all the time. Looking too hard. Guilt. Guilt makes her run—

JUSTIN: She's on a—

SOPHY: I know. A quest. Judaism has all of this. What she's looking for. She could find it in—

JUSTIN: I don't think it's her way.

SOPHY: Of course it's her way. She's a Jewish girl.

JUSTIN: Yes. But I think she has her own way. And, you know—

SOPHY: She hates me.

JUSTIN: She doesn't hate you.

SOPHY: She hates me because she still thinks I hate her.

JUSTIN: We didn't know you like we knew each other. You were older, and pretty—you went to those schools—

SOPHY: Thank God they finally sent me to those schools, that's all I can say. Getting high saved my ass, it got me out of that house—away from the fucking damage of—

JUSTIN: Yeah.

SOPHY: I feel old.

JUSTIN: You're not old.

SOPHY: I am. I'm like thirty-three.

JUSTIN: You're not old.

SOPHY: Guys don't look at me like they used to.

JUSTIN: *(Referring to her religiousgarb)* Um, maybe that's because you're wearing a wig and a tent?

SOPHY: Yeah. Maybe that's it.

*(*JUSTIN *and* SOPHY *laugh. Beat)*

SOPHY: I miss dancing.

JUSTIN: You do?

SOPHY: Yes. I don't feel special anymore. I want to take my clothes off and snort cocaine and feed the hungry. Sometimes they'd lick the window.

JUSTIN: More information than I needed—

SOPHY: I just have to keep it together. In these shoes, and tent, following the rules. I mean, Honey, I go out there. I go way out. Without anchors, I just like, float out and—

JUSTIN: I know.

SOPHY: Can you stop me? Can you put those fabulous sweet hands right here *(She shows him where; it is not sexual, but it disturbs him nonetheless. She is asking him to heal her.)* and keep me from floating out? Just once?

JUSTIN: No. I don't think I can. *(And then, to* MIRIAM*)* The last time I saw Sophy she said she didn't hate you, Miriam. And she asked me to save her. And I said no.

Twenty-two
A Love Letter To God

SOPHY: A love letter.

how You fed me. how You bathed me. how You got inside and found me right when i thought i was lost. how i'm not lost anymore. how You reminded me to hope. how You pulled me out of the past and put me right into the future. how You taught me to love. how, since You found me, we will never be apart.

my heart was submerged. but it isn't anymore.

i hope this lasts a long time, this part where everything is about You. Because right now everything is about You.

Twenty-three

TANGEE: Do you think we can know our purpose? Who we're supposed to be with and why? Do you think love is important?

RABBI: You ask a lot of questions.

TANGEE: Yes. I have a lot.

RABBI: You do. Well. Yes, I think love is important. Family too. It's a big part of our religion, family. Do I think we can know God's will? I think we can try. That's what's important to me. That we try.

TANGEE: I know what you mean.

RABBI: You do?

TANGEE: I do.

RABBI: It's all we have really. That we try.

TANGEE: I have this beautiful little girl. I didn't want her at first. I was too young. But she's here and I love her so much—I look at her and see how big the future is. And how vulnerable. It needs us to protect it. The future. My little girl.

RABBI: This is a beautiful thing.

TANGEE: It is. And my boyfriend, or whatever he is, is kinda psychic. His whole family is except for his parents who were just totally freaked and ran off to Scottsdale. I've never even met them. But no one can really know the future, can they? I mean, can they?

RABBI: I don't know. It's a good question. Not one I can answer.

TANGEE: Yeah. Me either. We think we know. But who knows what we think we know. I just want to protect the future.

RABBI: Or help it move along.

TANGEE: Sure.

RABBI: I think we know what we need to know when we need to kno it. A need-to-know basis.

TANGEE: Like in the spy movies.

RABBI: Exactly.

TANGEE: Hey, would you want to go out for coffee some time? Do they let you do that?

RABBI: Drink coffee?

TANGEE: With single mom shiksas.

RABBI: Oh. I think it would be fine.

TANGEE: Good. You can tell me more about embodied infinitely practical nontranscendent religion. Because

honestly I think the whole thing is totally fascinating.
How I Died

SOPHY: This is how I died: I just did. I got ready, and
I did. I could say it was suicide, only it wasn't. It was
more like a parade. A parade went by and I joined
it. I joined the parade. It was nothing spectacular or
dramatic. Or holy. It was quiet and it all slowed down
so much. I just got in line with the others and followed.
It was not an act of leadership. It was an act of
following. Of joining in. I just got in line. I had a great
hat. I wanted to show off my great hat. In the Parade.

Twenty-four

(JUSTIN *returns to the motel.* MIRIAM *is there waiting. Her
skin itches. She is spent, and emotionally and physically,
unexpectedly vulnerable.*)

JUSTIN: No luck.

MIRIAM: Where'd you go?

JUSTIN: Everywhere. The clubs. A couple of them. The
one I kept getting the most, it was—

MIRIAM: *(Intuiting)* She wasn't there.

JUSTIN: I talked to a bunch of the dancers. I bought
them drinks asked if they remembered her. I had a
picture—no one knew her. Nothing.

MIRIAM: They were lying. The one with the—she was
lying.

JUSTIN: Yeah. That girl—with the—she said she'd be
my cousin. She offered to take me in the back and be
my cousin. But I said no.

MIRIAM: Good.

JUSTIN: Then I went to Hillel House. And her shul.
And I said, I'm looking for my cousin. She's about this

tall and—I showed them the picture. They were very interested—just not in her. They were interested in me as a young Jewish male, a Son—our people, they have this fetish for "sons".

MIRIAM: Yeah. They love that shit.

JUSTIN: They too offered to take me in back—to pray, to teach me the many wonders of the Jewish world, the meaning hidden in repetition. Why does everyone have such an unwarranted stake in who I go out with? I said no. I only want to find my cousin.
      What's with your skin?

MIRIAM: I don't know.

JUSTIN: Is it excema?

MIRIAM: I don't know. It's fucking gross.

JUSTIN: Yeah. It is.

MIRIAM: Thanks.

JUSTIN: What do you do for that?

MIRIAM: I don't know.

JUSTIN: How do you treat it?

MIRIAM: I don't know.

JUSTIN: Well you should do something.

MIRIAM: Can't *you*?

JUSTIN: I don't know how.

MIRIAM: You do. You just won't. (*As if a big exhale*) You could just put your hands on my skin, and the itching would stop and the guilt would stop and the bullshit would stop, and you can, and I want you to. I want you to do all the things you know how to do, and none of them are wrong or bad, and none of it is what happened to Sophy.

(JUSTIN *doesn't say anything. He just watches* MIRIAM.)

MIRIAM *(Breaking)* I'm tired. I'm just so tired.
I want my fucking mother.

(JUSTIN says nothing. She, frustrated, gives up—)

JUSTIN: Come here.

(MIRIAM looks up at JUSTIN.)

MIRIAM: Why?

JUSTIN: I don't know.

MIRIAM: *(With none of her usual fight or spirit, she is depleted)* You come here.

(JUSTIN goes to MIRIAM.)

(JUSTIN and MIRIAM are still for a beat. Finally, he puts his hands on her face. Where the skin is flaking.)

JUSTIN: It's telling me things.

MIRIAM: What's it telling me? I mean, you? What's it telling you?

(JUSTIN whispers into MIRIAM's ear all the things her skin is telling him. And then he kisses her. In all the places where the skin is flaking—where she itches from guilt and sadness—and as they connect with each other, SOPHY's spirit releases back into the void. And there is peace.)

(SOPHY's final text may be overlaid with this, as if each touch presses her on to say what she has to so that she can go.... Every time MIRIAM and JUSTIN touch, SOPHY gets to speak a line—)

SOPHY: this is how i died.
baruch ata adonai—
a sex worker exchanges sexual energy for—
this is how i died.
the world stopped spinning. it did. it stopped and let me go, it let me go and i released it, the world, from my greedy little fingers, and floated up and then i saw everything, and now i'm here, in the in-between.

Waiting for you to send me through the gateways, waiting for Hashem to let me in upstairs, for my grandma, Magic Lena to open all the doors and tell me it's okay, and for the blackest most pure angels to show me how to release the pieces of the world i cling to. My grandma always said i cling.

I'm ready now. To move through.

(She crosses over.)

*(*MIRIAM *and* JUSTIN *hold one another.)*

Twenty-five
What Happened To Steve
An Interlude

(With radically different lighting)

STEVE: Well, after I got dropped off in Akron, all sorts of things started happening . For one thing, I got back in touch with my daughter. But that didn't happen first.

First I went to see a woman. Outside of Akron. Not that kind of woman. This was a family friend. She used to know my mom. I hadn't seen my mom in about twelve years. She was, well she left my dad a long time ago, back there in Abilene Texas. And for another, we just hadn't, we didn't get a long for a spell. And I needed something to come in and just stir it all up, this big crazy shit inside me. I had a lot of big crazy shit inside me. I still do have a lot of big crazy shit. Only now it's stirred up.

My daughter was less than a year when I left her mother. I couldn't stay. I wouldn't have been a good dad. My ex moved. We didn't talk. Til yesterday.

It was after that crazy chick with the truck. Miriam. Named after something in the Bible that I had never heard of. I wasn't even going to Akron—or Ohio at all—before her.

But she was going North through Ohio and I knew
Charlene in Akron, and so I went to see Charlene, the
woman who'd known my mom, and then—well, see
that girl was talking all about her mom having died,
and I hadn't talked to mine in some time, and seeing
Charlene stirred that up quite a bit, so I called her
and said something, I don't even know what I said,
but she asked me about Evelyn. My little girl. And
then, I had to tell my mom who I don't talk to much
all about how I'm not talking to my daughter much
on account of how her mother's still mad at me about
how the marriage, you know, broke apart, how I left,
the things I was saying back then (I think she still calls
me "Fuckhead") and there's this kid, Evelyn, with my
genes, she might even look like me, and I don 't see
her too much and I don't send money—Hell, I don't
make enough for me let alone to support Angela and
the girl—but really, really it's just because I'm scared.
I mean, that's all. It is just because I'm scared. And all
of those things started getting real clear to me. And so
I called Angela and asked if I could see my little girl.
Evelyn. We named her after, oh Hell I don't remember
what we named her after. But I'm headed there next.
To see my kid. My daughter.

Twenty-six

(MIRIAM and JUSTIN *leave the motel. They embrace and
then head in opposite directions.* MIRIAM *gets into her truck.*
JUSTIN *holds out his hand. And we move into the final scene
of the play.*)

Twenty-seven

(MIRIAM *sits in her truck with a new hitchhiker, a woman.*
The woman is played by the actress who played SOPHY.)

MIRIAM: I come from a line. The women in my
family. some of the men, too. My cousin justin. We
get messages and dreams. He can heal people. all of
us can. We know things. I never connected this line,
the gift we have, with heritage. But I have been told
there might be a connection. and I'm starting to think
about it. There are things about my own people that
I'm completely ignorant of. I am an American Jew,
and I come from this line of weird psychics, but I am
an American. And there is no past when you're an
American.

WOMAN: True.

MIRIAM: I want to find my people. And I don't even
know what that means.

(JUSTIN *is seen hitchiking. The* WOMAN *turns to him, as if
to let him into her car.*)

WOMAN: Hi.

JUSTIN: Thanks for picking me up. Where are you
going?

WOMAN: *(To* MIRIAM*)* What about the ones you left?

MIRIAM: I love them, both of them, more than I can say.

JUSTIN: My cousin died this week. And my girlfriend
left me for a Rabbi.

WOMAN: *(To* JUSTIN*)* Really?
(To MIRIAM*)* I'm Jewish.

MIRIAM: Really?

JUSTIN: And my other cousin, she's gone home, to our
house, I kept it, our family house, and she's going

there. I don't know. A lot's disrupted. What do you know about the desert?

WOMAN: *(To* MIRIAM*)* We're a people in exile. What do you suppose are the lessons of a people in exile?

MIRIAM: We all just want to go home.

JUSTIN: I have these dreams sometimes—that I'm in the midst of a great war or a siege and people are dying and I'm dying too—and then something always happens in the dream to make me remember. and once I remember that I have this power, I'm able to stop the dream. I think this is called lucid dreaming. but I remember and I stop the action of the dream and open my eyes, back inside themselves, and the screen, because it's like a huge screen, is flooded with light. I remember that I'm able to invoke light and I do, and the killing stops.

MIRIAM: We all just want to go home.

END OF PLAY

www.ingramcontent.com/pod-product-compliance
Lightning Source LLC
Chambersburg PA
CBHW070028110426
42741CB00034B/2684